The Library of Subatomic Particles™

The Photon

Fred Bortz

The Rosen Publishing Group, Inc., New York

To Susan, for the light she brings to my life

Published in 2004 by The Rosen Publishing Group, Inc.
29 East 21st Street, New York, NY 10010

Library of Congress Cataloging-in-Publication Data

Bortz, Alfred B.
The photon / Fred Bortz.— 1st ed.
    v. cm. — (The library of subatomic particles)
Includes bibliographical references and index.
Contents: The nature of light—Discovering the photon—Photons and atoms—Photons in technology.
ISBN 0-8239-4531-6 (lib. bdg.)
1. Photons—Juvenile literature. [1. Photons. 2. Light.]
I. Title. II. Series.
QC793.5.P42B67 2004
539.7'217—dc21

2003009181

Manufactured in the United States of America

On the cover: Inside the tube of a laser, excited atoms emit photons of coherent light.

Contents

Introduction

This book is unlike the others in The Library of Subatomic Particles in an important way, but it is connected to them in even more important ways. Instead of telling the story of a particle of matter, this book tells about a bundle of pure energy, a particle with no mass at all that always zips along at exactly the speed of light. Max Planck, the scientist who first proposed it in 1900, called it a quantum (plural, quanta). He didn't think quanta were real, but they made his mathematical formula work.

Five years later, Albert Einstein, explaining a phenomenon called the photoelectric effect, convinced people that Planck's quanta actually existed. For more than a century before that, science had been certain that light consisted of waves. Now, thanks to Einstein's insights, light was known to behave—under certain circumstances—not as a wave but like a stream of particles called photons.

Before Einstein's work, physics had made clear-cut distinctions between waves and particles. The discovery of the photon blurred the difference. Along with the earlier discovery of the electron and the later discovery of the nucleus, it opened the door to a new understanding of atoms and shed light on the nature of matter itself.

We now know that atoms are swarming with subatomic particles. They absorb photons, produce photons, and would not stay together without photons, yet they don't "contain" photons in the usual sense of that word.

All that adds an air of mystery to this journey inside matter and energy. It will follow paths of investigation about photons, and it will lead to many useful devices made possible by the knowledge discovered along the way.

Chapter One

The Nature of Light

What is light? That simple question has driven human curiosity for as long as our brains have been smart enough to wonder about the world in which we find ourselves. It has also led scientists to many unexpected discoveries, not only about the nature of light but also about the nature of matter and the forces that govern the universe.

The Visible Spectrum

Among the first to pursue that question were two seventeenth-century scientists who are considered to be among the most important of their time—or of any time: Sir Isaac Newton (1642–1727) and Christiaan Huygens (1629–1695).

At Cambridge University in England in the mid-1660s, the young Newton made some important observations about color.

Until that time, the prevailing scientific view was that white light was pure, and something had to be added to produce color. Though that theory fit with common sense, Newton discovered that it was wrong.

In a darkened room with a hole in the window shade that allowed a sunbeam to enter, Newton took a piece of glass in the

Colorful Physicist. By experimenting with light passing through glass prisms, Isaac Newton established that white light was a mixture of all the colors of the spectrum. He also theorized that light was a stream of particles he called corpuscles.

shape of a triangular prism and put it in the beam's path. The light emerged from the prism in a different direction, and it spread out much more than it would have without the prism. More important, when the light struck the opposite wall, it was no longer white. Instead, Newton observed a band of colors from red to violet, like those of a rainbow.

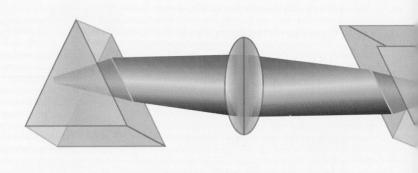

Newton's Prisms. Newton discovered that white light was actually a mixture of all colors by passing a beam of sunlight through a glass prism. Each color refracted at a slightly different angle, and thus they spread out into a band of colors called a spectrum. When he passed all the colors of that band through a second prism, identical to the first but upside down, the colors came back together as white light.

Newton had expected the change of direction (called refraction), since many people had observed that phenomenon when light entered water or glass at an angle. But where did the colors come from? The glass was clear, and furthermore, when sunlight passed through a flat piece of glass, it remained white.

Newton investigated by putting a second prism, identical to the first but with its angle reversed, in the path of the refracted light. If the second prism caught the light of all the spread-out colors, then the colors came together and white light emerged. If the second prism captured only one color, then only that color and

Doing the Wave. Unlike Newton, Christiaan Huygens believed light was a wave. The wave-or-particle question proved to be a very important one in understanding both light and matter.

no other appeared on the other side.

Soon the significance of Newton's results became clear. White light is not pure but rather a mixture of all colors from red to violet, which Newton called the spectrum. Today we call it the visible spectrum, because we know that the colors that we are able to see are not all the colors that nature has to offer. Beyond the ends of the visible spectrum, sunlight contains infrared and ultraviolet light.

Waves or Particles?

But what is light made of? Because it travels in straight lines and casts sharp shadows, and because its beams reflect from mirrors like a ball bouncing off a hard floor, Newton decided

Refraction of Particles

To understand how a stream of corpuscles or particles can refract, try this project. Take a wide piece of stiff cardboard, such as a poster board, and support one end of it on a stack of books so it becomes a ramp leading down to a hard floor.

Now take a marble or a similar-sized hard, small ball and roll it down the ramp, not straight along the center but at an angle. When the ball crosses from the ramp to the floor, notice that it changes direction.

A similar change in direction takes place when light passes from air to glass or water, an effect you may have discovered for yourself if you ever dove into a swimming pool to pick up an object at the bottom only to discover that your target is not where you expected it to be.

that light must be made of tiny particles, which he called corpuscles.

Across the North Sea in the Netherlands, however, Christiaan Huygens was more comfortable with the idea that light was a wave. In his mind, the refraction of light was a phenomenon similar to the way ocean waves, heading toward shore, change direction when they cross a submerged sandbar at an angle.

But how can waves cast sharp shadows? Huygens explained that if the wavelength— the distance from one crest, or peak, to the next—is much smaller than the object the waves are passing, the shadow will be sharp. For instance, when ocean waves approach a very large ship from one side, there is a calm region on the opposite side. The larger the ship or the closer together the crests, the farther the calm region extends. In other words, the shadow is sharper since the waves don't fill it in as much.

So Huygens proposed that light is made of waves with wavelengths that were too small too detect, while Newton spoke of undetectable tiny corpuscles. Both theories could explain all known properties of light at that time, and both men were long dead before anyone came up with an experiment that might settle the wave-particle question for good. That experiment took place in 1801, and the person who did it was English physicist Thomas Young (1773–1829). Young created a narrow sunbeam by passing sunlight through a pinhole. He then split the beam in two with a piece of thin cardboard placed edgewise. Instead of casting a sharp, thin shadow, as would be expected if the card had divided a stream of particles, the split beam produced a series of light and dark bands—an effect called interference. Interference occurs when waves meet. Where two peaks or two troughs meet, the result is a higher peak or deeper trough, which corresponds to brighter light. Where a peak meets a trough, they cancel each other, which results in darkness.

Young's experiment proved once and for all that light was a wave phenomenon—or so scientists thought at the time. But that discovery opened up new questions. A particle might travel through empty space, but surely a wave needs a medium to wiggle in, scientists thought. So they invented something called the aether, and they concluded that it filled all space, even though it had never been detected. (If you're having trouble imagining what the aether might be like, don't worry. It turns out that light waves don't need anything to wiggle in. The aether doesn't exist. That explains why

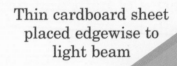

Thin cardboard sheet
placed edgewise to
light beam

Cardboard sheet
with pinhole

Light Source

Pattern of Proof. A famous experiment by Thomas Young in 1801 seemed to settle the wave-or-particle question for light once and for all. He split a narrow light beam into two parts, but instead of producing two separate spots, the beams produced a pattern of alternating light and dark spots called an interference pattern, which results when two waves overlap.

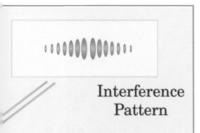

Interference
Pattern

scientists could never detect it.)

Maxwell's Mathematics

One physicist who believed in the aether was James Clerk Maxwell (1831–1879). In 1856, he began his career as a professor at Marischal College in the city of Aberdeen in his native Scotland. Mathematical by nature, he began researching ways to describe electricity, magnetism, and the relationships between the two in mathematical terms.

Though his work in Aberdeen showed promise, his ideas did not come together fully until soon after he moved to King's

Electromagnetic Math. James Clerk Maxwell described the relationship between electricity and magnetism by a set of four mathematical equations. When combined, those equations predicted electromagnetic waves that traveled through space at a speed equal to that measured for light. With that result, scientists were certain not only that light was a wave but also what kind of wave it was.

College in London in 1860. By 1861, he had written down a set of four equations that are now among the most famous in science.

Not only did Maxwell's equations describe the relationships between electric and magnetic fields, but they also paid an unexpected dividend. They suggested that a wave of electromagnetism could travel through space and even produced a formula for what the speed of such a wave would be. Astonishingly, that speed was almost exactly the same as the most recently measured speed of light. Thanks to Maxwell's work, physicists now knew not only that light was a wave phenomenon as shown by Young's experiment, but they also believed they knew what kind of a wave it was. The aether, even though it had never been observed in any way, carried both electricity and magnetism. Or did it? Though Maxwell's writings described his view that electromagnetic waves traveled through the aether, his equations did not include anything that described the properties of that mysterious whatever-it-was.

Some physicists saw something in Maxwell's equations that Maxwell himself did not. Or perhaps it is better to say that they saw nothing where Maxwell assumed that something was needed. They argued that electric and magnetic fields could satisfy Maxwell's equations without an aether or anything else to support them, so why invent something that no one can detect? They were right, but it took more than forty years of scientific progress until the famous theory of relativity ended the discussion in 1905. (The details of that story are interesting, but they belong in another book.)

Even if physicists disagreed about whether there was an aether, they no longer argued about the nature of light. Sixty years earlier, Young had demonstrated the truth of Huygens's theory of light as a wave phenomenon; and now Maxwell's mathematics had shown that those waves were electromagnetic.

It was time to move ahead—to learn more about the way matter and electromagnetic waves interacted. No one suspected that as they followed their investigations, Newton's corpuscular theory of light would be reborn, or that the corpuscles, called photons, would be central to a new understanding of both electromagnetism and the nature of matter.

Chapter Two

Discovering the Photon

At the same time that Maxwell was discovering the electromagnetic nature of light, other scientists were exploring the atomic nature of matter. The existence of atoms was still very much in the realm of theory, but the evidence was mounting that atoms were real. The way substances reacted chemically and the way gases behaved when heated or put under pressure fit with the theory that matter was composed of tiny particles in constant motion.

Among the scientists who believed in atoms were those who worked in thermodynamics, the branch of physics dealing with heat and temperature. They found that the best way to understand heat was by considering it the internal energy of matter due to the incessant motion of its atoms. Maxwell himself made major contributions to these developing ideas.

Hot Body Spectra and Planck's Dilemma

Quanta in the Glow.
Max Planck developed a mathematical model of the spectrum produced by a hot body based on the radiation from its vibrating atoms. To make his model agree with measurements, he introduced the idea of packets of light energy called quanta, which he considered to be a mathematical device with no physical significance.

One of the questions those scientists wondered about concerned the glow produced when an object is heated. How do hot objects transform their heat energy—the motion of their atoms—into light, that is, electromagnetic waves? Could they explain how, as its temperature rises, a heated body's glow gets brighter and its color changes from deep red, to brighter red, to orange and yellow?

In 1895, the renowned professor Max Planck (1858–1947) at the University of Berlin in Germany turned his theoretical skills to that question. Could he come up with a formula that described the spectrum—the mixture of different colors of light—that radiates from hot bodies? Using a spectrometer, a device that spreads light into its component colors like a prism, scientists had observed the light that came from holes cut into the sides of very hot furnaces. Planck looked at the graphs of their experimental data, showing how the brightness varied for each color in the glow, and tried to find a formula that would match the curves he saw there in every detail.

To represent a color mathematically, Planck used its corresponding frequency (how fast the electromagnetic wave wiggles), increasing for visible light from the lowest frequency at the red end of the spectrum to the highest frequency at the violet end. He even used measurements of invisible light in the infrared (below red) and ultraviolet (above violet) regions.

Planck looked at graphs for different temperatures and noted that all had one important common feature. Starting from infrared and going toward ultraviolet, they would rise to a peak and then fall toward zero. As temperatures rose, the light was more intense, and the peaks of the graphs were higher. The peak also shifted toward higher frequencies as the temperature rose, corresponding to the changing color of the furnaces from deep red to bright red to orange to yellow. But no matter how hot the furnaces got, the measured intensity always dropped off sharply beyond the peak.

Planck thought about what kind of a model he could use to represent a hot radiating body. It had to lead to a formula he could use to make a prediction about its spectrum. He settled on modeling the furnace as a collection of vibrating atoms, each producing electromagnetic waves according to Maxwell's formulas. He added those waves together to produce a spectrum and graphed it. His calculations yielded a remarkable match to actual data at the low-frequency end. But in the ultraviolet region, instead of dropping off after reaching a peak, the formula predicted an ever-rising intensity of light.

Planck struggled to find a fix for the problem and finally came up with what he considered a mathematical trick. What if energy was not like a fluid that could be

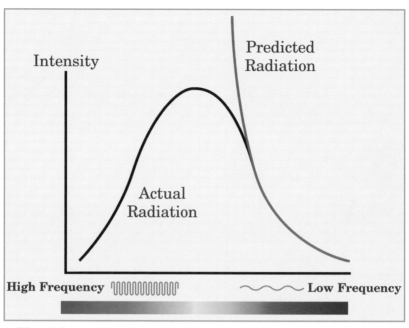

The "Ultraviolet Catastrophe." This diagram shows why Planck invented the quantum. The graph, going from left to right, shows the intensity of radiation in each color range (frequency) from ultraviolet to infrared. The lower curve is the measured spectrum of a white-hot body with the color reaching its peak intensity in the yellow range. The upper curve shows the result of Planck's model without the quantum—an excellent fit to the measurements at the infrared end but a "catastrophe" in the ultraviolet region. Adding the quantum produced a match between the theory and measurements at all frequencies and temperatures.

measured out in any amount but instead came in discrete chunks—which he called quanta (singular, quantum)—like grains of sand? Each atom could vibrate with zero, one, two, or three quanta of energy, and so forth; but nothing was allowed in between the whole numbers, such

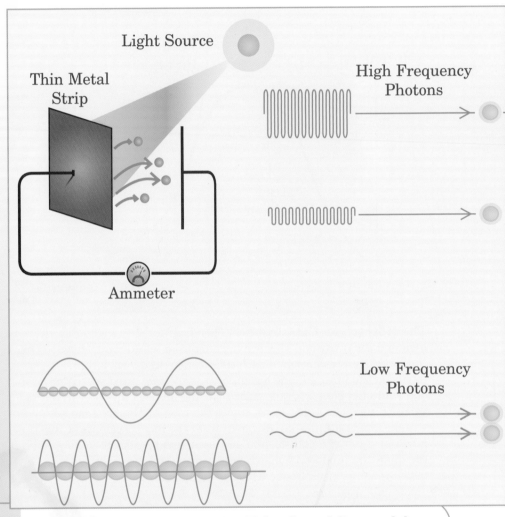

The Puzzle of Photoelectricity. Philipp Lenard discovered the photoelectric effect in which light beams knock electrons free from certain metals. The frequency of the light must be greater than a certain threshold value—usually in the violet or ultraviolet range—that is different for each metal. In this drawing, the two light beams at the top have the same high frequency (above the threshold), though one beam is much dimmer than the other. Nevertheless, both are capable of freeing electrons from the metal. The beam at the bottom is of a color below the threshold and thus fails to free electrons, even when it is very intense.

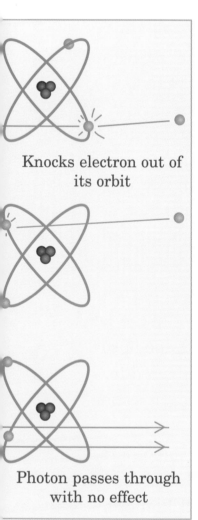

Knocks electron out of
its orbit

Photon passes through
with no effect

as a third of a quantum, two and one-half quanta, or 17.76 quanta.

Planck realized that he needed small quanta at low frequencies, where his formulas were fine. Small quanta wouldn't change the results, he reasoned, since you can measure out almost any volume of very fine sand. But at high frequencies, large quanta— more like a pile of pebbles than grains of sand—would limit the possible vibrations and perhaps explain the fall off in light intensity at high frequencies.

Planck began with the simplest approach. He calculated the spectrum, presuming a constant ratio between the quantum's energy and its frequency.

Doubling the frequency would double the quantum's energy. Multiplying the frequency by three would triple the energy of the quantum, and so forth.

For each temperature, Planck adjusted the ratio between the energy and the frequency of the quantum to match the calculated peak intensity to the observed peak of the spectrum. He hoped that by matching the highest point on each graph, the rest of the curve would also match fairly well, but the results astonished him. Not only did the peak intensity match, but so did the shape of the entire graph, all the way from infrared to ultraviolet. Even more surprising, the same ratio that made the curve fit for one temperature also worked for all the others.

Planck published the news of that amazing ratio, which today physicists call Planck's constant, in 1900. What began as a mathematical trick produced one of nature's fundamental values. But what did it mean? He and other physicists were determined to find out.

Einstein and the Photoelectric Effect

The explanation came from an unexpected direction, a puzzling phenomenon known as the photoelectric effect. While Planck was pondering quanta, another German physicist named Philipp Lenard (1862–1947) had discovered that shining light on a metal could cause an electric current to flow—but only under the right conditions.

The current was a stream of electrons, themselves newly discovered in 1897 and the only subatomic particles known at the time of Lenard's research. Each metal had a particular threshold frequency for the light. At colors more toward the red end of the spectrum, that is, those having a frequency below the threshold, the metal did not give up its electrons, no matter how intense the light. At higher frequencies, even the dimmest light would free some electrons. For most metals, that threshold was in the violet or ultraviolet range. But why should there be a threshold frequency at all?

In 1905, a little-known patent clerk in Switzerland named Albert Einstein (1879–1955) figured it out. Einstein knew that the minimum amount of energy needed to free an electron—the photoelectric threshold—varied from one metal to another. The threshold reminded him of a different phenomenon requiring a minimum amount of energy, Planck's quantum and the radiation of hot

One Answer to Two Questions. Albert Einstein described how the photoelectric effect could be understood if Planck's quanta (the bundles of energy we now call photons) were real instead of a mere mathematical trick. He thus answered two questions at once. But he also reopened a controversy that everyone thought Young's experiment had settled more than a century earlier. Is light a stream of particles or a wave?

bodies. Einstein realized that if quanta were not merely mathematical conveniences but real packets of light energy, they could explain the photoelectric threshold. These energetic bundles, which he called photons, would not join together like a group of people to lift a heavy load. Rather, Einstein explained, a photon either has enough energy to knock out an electron all by itself, or the electron stays put.

Below the threshold frequency, no matter how many photons are in the beam—that is, no matter how intense the light—each photon simply lacks the energy needed to knock an electron free from the metal. Above that threshold, even a single photon has enough energy to free an electron, so even the dimmest light of that color can free electrons.

By claiming that photons were real, however, Einstein raised an even bigger question. Thanks to Young's experiment more than a century earlier, everyone knew that light was not composed of a lumpy stream of particles, but consisted of smooth and steady waves. Sixty years after that, Maxwell's equations had identified the waves as electromagnetic, and the wave-or-particle question had a clear answer.

Now Einstein did not merely reopen that old controversy, but he changed the form of the question from "either-or." Sometimes light was an electromagnetic wave and sometimes it was a stream of photons—or perhaps, somehow, it was both at once!

Chapter Three

Photons and Atoms

How could light be made of waves in some cases and particles in others? Scientists found the explanation in an unexpected place—the internal structure of the atom. Since 1897, when J. J. Thomson (1856–1940) announced his discovery of the electron, physicists had puzzled about its tiny mass. What makes up the rest of atoms, they wondered, and how do the parts of atoms fit together? By 1911, the best measurements had determined that the electron's mass was approximately 1/1800th of that of the lightest atom (hydrogen). The work of the New Zealand-born Manchester University professor Ernest Rutherford (1871–1937) had revealed the surprising fact that the atom was mostly empty space, and most of its mass was concentrated in a compact tiny nucleus.

Rutherford described the atom as a miniature solar system with the nucleus as the Sun and the electrons as planets orbiting around it, held in place by electrical forces rather than gravity. But Rutherford's model had one very serious problem. According to Maxwell's equations, the orbiting electrons would radiate electromagnetic waves. That would cause them to lose energy and spiral into the nucleus. Rutherford's planetary model was unstable.

Connecting Photons to Atoms. Niels Bohr developed a model of the atom that depended on electrons occupying only certain allowed orbits around the nucleus, each orbit corresponding to a particular energy level. If an electron drops from a higher to a lower energy level, the atom emits a photon of a particular frequency. In the reverse process, an atom can also absorb a photon of that frequency, causing an electron in that lower energy level to jump to a higher one.

Line Spectra and the Bohr Atom

In 1913, Danish physicist Niels Bohr (1885–1962) found a way out of the instability problem, and it involved the photon. He was trying to understand the spectra produced when electricity

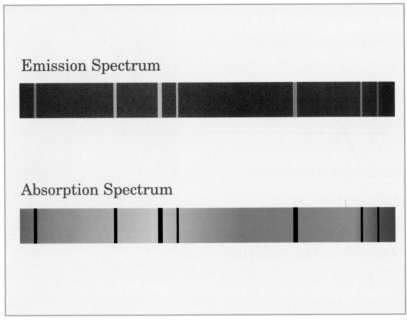

Emission Spectrum

Absorption Spectrum

Reading the Lines. Bohr's model of the hydrogen atom successfully predicted the line spectrum—the set of particular frequencies— emitted when that gas is electrically excited in a tube. That is called the emission line spectrum, the upper of the two spectra shown here. The lower band is the corresponding absorption spectrum, showing the same colors as dark bands at frequencies absorbed by hydrogen gas when sunlight passes through it.

passed through tubes filled with particular gases. Using devices called spectroscopes that separated the colors from the glowing tubes more than a prism could, scientists had discovered that the light from those tubes was quite different from the continuous band of colors that Newton had seen in sunlight. They saw instead a series of sharp lines separated by darkness. The gases glowed only at very particular wavelengths.

The hydrogen spectrum was particularly interesting because it contained several sets of colored lines in which the wavelengths obeyed a simple mathematical relationship. Since the hydrogen atom was uncomplicated—just one electron in orbit around

Electrons as Waves. The Bohr model of the atom was built on an idea by Louis-Victor de Broglie, who said that if light could be both particles and waves at the same time, then so could matter, such as electrons.

a nucleus—Bohr hoped to develop a theory from the hydrogen spectrum that would uncover the physical phenomena underlying the mathematical patterns.

Bohr made some shrewd guesses about electron orbits. He began by accepting the French physicist Louis-Victor de Broglie's (1892–1987) extension of Einstein's interpretation of the photoelectric effect. If light waves have particle-like characteristics, then subatomic particles could likewise have wavelike characteristics.

Bohr started with de Broglie's formula for the relationship between the wavelength of electrons and their energy. He proposed that electrons have certain natural orbits, each with its own energy level, in which they would not radiate despite the predictions of Maxwell's equations. The distance around those special orbits was an exact number of wavelengths. Further, Bohr proposed that when an electron drops from one orbit to another with lower energy, the energy difference appears as a photon. Finally, Bohr calculated the frequencies of light that would result from hydrogen's natural orbits, and the results matched the observed lines in the hydrogen spectrum.

With Bohr's insight, the planetary model of the atom was making more sense. But it required scientists to revamp some of their most basic ideas, including eliminating the sharp distinction between particles and waves for the electron as well as the photon.

Quantum Mechanics

Now that Bohr's model had blurred the distinction between particles and waves, physicists needed a new way to understand the laws of electromagnetism and motion within the atom. Austrian professor Erwin Schrödinger (1887–1961) developed an equation that, instead of describing a particle as if it is in one place, substituted a mathematical formula called a wave function, which described the probability of finding the particle in many different places. Schrödinger's approach launched a new field of physics called quantum mechanics.

To understand what the wave function represents, imagine an object bouncing back and forth on a tight spring so fast that all you can see is a blur. The blur is darkest near the ends of its motion where the object moves more slowly as it decelerates and changes direction, and it is least distinct in the middle where it is moving fastest. But where is the object, really? That's the wrong question to ask in quantum mechanics. All the equation can tell you is that the object is more likely to be

A Sharp Idea from Fuzzy Thinking. Erwin Schrödinger devised a mathematical way to represent the position of particles not as sharply defined places but rather as fuzzy clouds called wave functions. This approach opened up a new branch of physics called quantum mechanics.

found near an end than in the middle, because the object is the blur!

Schrödinger applied his equation to the hydrogen atom, and it produced a series of different wave functions—quantum states—that an electron might occupy. Each wave function was concentrated at a certain distance from the nucleus and was associated with a particular energy level. The distances and energy levels were exactly the ones that Bohr had calculated. But quantum mechanics had one significant advantage over the Bohr model. It didn't require changing the laws of electromagnetism for special orbits. Instead, it led people to a new view of electrons in atoms. Rather than being particles following particular orbits, they were fuzzy wave-function clouds occupying one of many "orbitals" within the atom.

The prediction of the hydrogen spectrum was the first of many theoretical triumphs for quantum mechanics, so physicists gradually accepted this new blurry view of subatomic particles. In Germany, Werner Heisenberg (1901–1976) realized that quantum mechanical ideas had great significance for understanding measurement. When scientists measure something, the precision of their instruments is always limited, and the number they get is never perfectly exact. They will say the measurement has an uncertainty.

Heisenberg realized that minimizing the uncertainty in the

The Certainty of Uncertainty. Werner Heisenberg recognized that quantum mechanics had important implications about the limits of measurement, which he expressed in mathematical terms as the uncertainty principle.

measured position of an object depends on how well you know its speed. Likewise, minimizing the uncertainty in the measured speed depends on how well you know where it is. He soon realized that the two minimum uncertainties were related—their product was Planck's constant divided by the mass of the object—and that quantum mechanics was nature's way of describing the limits on how well the two related quantities could be measured. Heisenberg found a similar result for the measurement of time intervals and energy.

Quantum Electrodynamics and "Virtual" Photons

The Heisenberg uncertainty principle also turns out to be very important for understanding electromagnetic effects within atoms. Maxwell's equations had been developed to describe the electrical and magnetic interactions between particles whose location could be precisely measured. The equations described electric and magnetic fields that vary precisely in space and time according to certain mathematical rules.

Inside the atom, quantum mechanical fuzziness made such precision impossible.

To understand photons and other subatomic particles, scientists needed to replace Maxwell's equations, which were the basis of an area of physics called electrodynamics, with a new mathematical formulation called quantum electrodynamics, or QED. The problem, physicists discovered, was that they needed a new mathematical vocabulary to express nature's language for QED. It was not until the late 1940s that American physicist Richard Feynman (1918–1988) of the California Institute of Technology came up with a language of symbols for QED, which are known today as Feynman diagrams.

Feynman's work also changed some basic notions about matter, energy, and nothingness, which physicists call "the vacuum." You have probably learned that energy can change forms but cannot be created or destroyed. (You may have even learned that mass is also a form of energy.) Physicists call that the law of conservation of energy. But how can anyone be sure that energy hasn't appeared or disappeared without measuring it? The uncertainty principle

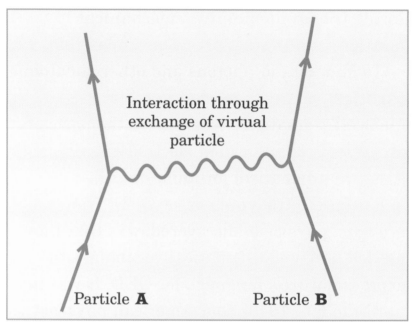

Interaction through exchange of virtual particle

Particle **A**   Particle **B**

The Language of QED. How can the exactness of Maxwell's equations of electromagnetism fit with the fuzziness of the quantum world? That was the question physicists struggled with as they developed the theory of quantum electrodynamics (QED). They eventually devised a theory that relied on Feynman diagrams like this one, named after the physicist who first drew them.

forced physicists to say that if you measure energy for a very, very short time, the uncertainty in the measurement must be very, very large.

Feynman described it this way: The vacuum is not perfect emptiness. Rather, it is full of "virtual" photons and particles that flicker into

Photons and Electromagnetic Forces

The way physicists apply Feynman's ideas to electromagnetism is easy to illustrate but difficult to compute. The Feynman diagram *(opposite)* shows two electrons labeled A and B moving along straight paths from bottom to top. At a certain time, electron A emits a virtual photon (the wiggly line), and that causes it to lose energy and change its direction of motion. A short time later, electron B absorbs that photon, gaining energy and also changing its direction. Between the emission and absorption events, the universe gained a bit of energy, but that energy disappeared too quickly to be detected. That virtual event causes the electrons to repel each other, just as particles with like charges ought to do.

and out of existence so quickly that any appearance or disappearance of energy is undetectable according to the uncertainty principle. The electromagnetic force is the result of the interactions between electrically charged particles and those virtual photons.

Feynman and other physicists worked out the ways to add up all possible exchanges of virtual photons between charged particles, producing a theory of QED that not only fit with Maxwell's equations for large bodies, but also worked for subatomic particles. More important, that understanding of QED led to a new way of thinking about photons. They were not only particles of electromagnetic energy like light, but they were also the carriers of the electromagnetic interaction between subatomic particles—including the electrical forces that bind electrons to their nuclei.

Chapter Four

Photons in Technology

How important is it in everyday life to know whether light is made of waves or particles? The answer, in a word, is the laser. Lasers and other high-technology devices rely on our understanding of the interactions between light and matter—between photons and atoms. Let's look at the fields of spectroscopy and crystallography.

Hydrogen is not the only substance to have a distinctive line spectrum. Each atom or molecule has a unique set of energy levels, which means that each produces a line spectrum that is different from any other. Not only do they have emission line spectra that result from electrons dropping from a higher energy level to a lower one, emitting a photon in the process, but they also have absorption spectra that occur when photons are absorbed and boost electrons from lower

The Light Decides. The technician in this picture is using a high-resolution spectrometer to analyze minute samples of chemical substances. The instrument records and analyzes the spectrum of light energy, from infrared to X-ray wavelengths, that is emitted when the chemicals become incandescent.

energy levels to higher ones. Thus chemists have devised a variety of spectroscopes (instruments that spread light into the light's spectrum) and spectrometers (instruments that measure spectra) to identify the atoms or molecules in a sample by the line spectra that they emit or absorb.

Those spectral lines occur not only in visible light, but also in electromagnetic waves with longer or shorter wavelengths, depending on the difference between energy levels. These include infrared light and microwaves at longer wavelengths and ultraviolet light and X-rays at shorter wavelengths.

In the long-wavelength spectra, the energy levels are often not determined by electron orbits but rather by other properties of matter. For example, molecules of a gas or liquid are free to spin around, but quantum mechanics tells us that the spinning rate can only take on certain values. Thus there are rotational energy levels, and the molecules emit or absorb photons whose energy corresponds to transitions between their different states of rotation. Likewise, because the bonds between atoms in a molecule can act like miniature springs, there are energy levels that correspond to different rates of atomic vibration. Those occur in solids as well as liquids and gases.

Looking at the photons that result from transitions between different rotational or vibrational energy levels, chemists are often

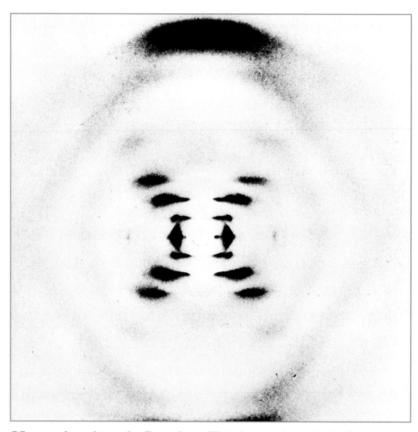

Measuring Atomic Spacing. This image is an interference pattern produced by X-rays reflecting from a crystalline solid. It was made in 1953 by Rosalind Franklin and shows the molecular structure of DNA. The bands reveal the arrangement and spacing between atomic layers and of the atoms within those layers.

able to deduce important information about chemical bonding in different substances. That knowledge can guide them in their search for important new materials.

X-ray photons are also important tools for chemists and physicists. When an electron makes a transition between nearby energy levels, the photon produced or absorbed is usually in or near the range of visible light. But sometimes a high-energy event like a sudden collision of a fast-moving particle with an atom causes an electron to make a transition between two very widely separated energy levels, producing an X-ray photon that is characteristic of that particular atom. Scientists use X-ray emission spectroscopy to study the chemical composition of a sample material on a microscopic scale, and that is often important for understanding whether that sample is suitable for use in a high-technology device or in explaining why a particular device failed.

Because X-rays have higher frequencies, or shorter wavelengths, than visible light, they are not only more penetrating, but they can reveal finer microscopic detail. Beams of X-rays are useful in crystallography, the study of the repetitive arrangement of atoms within a solid. The X-rays reflect from crystals and produce patterns on photographic plates that enable scientists to determine the spacing between layers of atoms and the arrangement of those atoms within layers. That knowledge is important for making and understanding new materials.

Lasers

The best-known technological achievement that depends on photons is the laser. Ordinary light of a particular color is made of many waves with the same spacing between their crests and troughs, but with the crests of one wave in no particular relationship to the crests of any other. Laser light is different from ordinary light and much more powerful because every wave is in perfect crest-to-crest alignment. Five unmatched waves produce a beam five times as intense as any one of them, but five perfectly matched waves produce a sharp and powerful beam twenty-five times more intense (five times five) that hardly spreads out at all.

How does a laser produce such a beam? It is the result of a phenomenon called stimulated

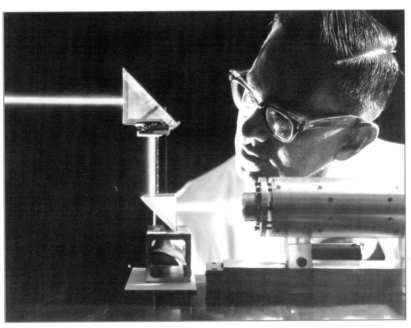

A Laser Gazer. Being careful not to look directly into the laser beam, this man is studying the operation of an early laser. In 1965, when this picture was taken, lasers were rare, expensive, and usually about the size shown here. Today they are common, with a wide range of size, power, and cost. Laser applications include medicine, manufacturing, military, computing, communication, and entertainment.

emission of radiation that occurs when a photon of a particular energy interacts with an atom. Suppose the atom would normally emit such a photon when one of its electrons drops from a higher energy level, called the excited state, to its lowest possible energy level, called the ground state. If a photon of that energy

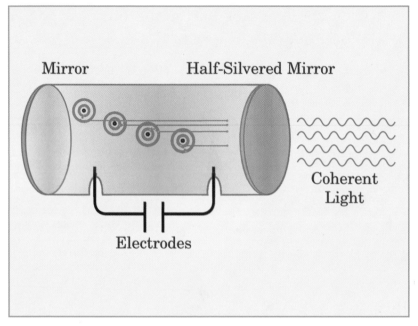

Photons on Parade. The word "laser" stands for light amplification by stimulated emission of radiation. The process begins by
exciting the electrons of a large number of atoms. When one atom
spontaneously emits a photon, that photon stimulates other atoms
to emit photons of the same energy (frequency) so that all belong to
waves with crests and troughs in perfect alignment, producing a
powerful burst of light with a precise color and a precise direction.

meets an atom with an electron in the ground
state, that electron might absorb the photon's
energy and jump up to the excited state. Once
in the excited state, the electron would stay for
a while before dropping back and emitting a
photon just like the one it absorbed. That's
called spontaneous emission.

But what happens when a photon of that energy meets an atom where the electron is already in the excited state? You might think that nothing unusual would take place, that the excited electron would drop back down and emit a photon at the same time as it would have ordinarily emitted a photon, but that is not true. Instead of spontaneously emitting a photon at an unpredictable time, the electron reacts to the passing photon by dropping down and emitting a second photon in perfect alignment with the first, as if the two were members of a marching band in perfect step.

Now if one of those photons encounters another electron in the excited state, it stimulates that electron to drop down, and a third photon joins the parade. In a laser, an energy source excites electrons in many atoms in the same material at the same time. Then as soon as one drops to its ground state and spontaneously emits a photon, a rapid chain reaction of stimulated emissions begins. In a flash (in both senses of the word), most of the atoms emit their photons in perfect alignment with each other.

Seeing Infrared. These night-vision goggles enable the wearer to see heat radiation—infrared light—by absorbing it in materials that then emit visible light. To develop those materials, scientists and engineers needed to understand the quantum mechanical behavior of photons.

That's light amplification by stimulated emission of radiation, the process that gives lasers their name. Laser light has many applications in technology because its beams can be very sharp and powerful and yet are easy to modify and control.

Other important technologies rely on the interactions between photons and atoms. For example, night-vision goggles rely on materials that absorb photons from infrared light to raise already excited electrons to an even higher energy state, from which they quickly drop down to a ground state and emit visible light. Making materials with just the right set of energy levels for this to happen requires knowledge of the quantum mechanical behavior of semiconductors and the quantum nature of subatomic particles like the photon.

Glossary

absorption Taking in something from the surroundings, such as the absorption of a photon by an atom, resulting in the transition of an electron from a lower to a higher energy level.

atom The smallest bit of matter than can be identified as a certain chemical element.

compound A substance made of only one kind of molecule that consists of more than one kind of atom. For example, water is made of molecules that contain two atoms of hydrogen and one atom of oxygen.

electrodynamics A field of physics that describes the interactions and movement of particles due to electromagnetism.

electromagnetic wave A form of energy resulting from the interrelationship of changing electric and magnetic fields that flows through space at the speed of light.

electromagnetism A fundamental force of nature, or property of matter and energy, that includes electricity, magnetism, and electromagnetic waves, such as light.

electron A very light subatomic particle (the first to be discovered) that carries negative charge and is responsible for many important properties of matter.

element A substance made of only one kind of atom.

emission Sending out something that has been produced, such as the emission of a photon from an atom when an electron drops from a higher to a lower energy level.

energy level One of many values of energy that quantum mechanics permits for a physical phenomenon, such as for the allowed states of an electron in an atom.

interference A phenomenon that occurs when two waves meet, resulting in some regions of higher intensity and some of lower intensity, in particular the light and dark bands produced when two light waves meet.

laser A device that produces a sharp, powerful beam of light by the process known as light amplification through stimulated emission of radiation.

molecule The smallest bit of matter that can be identified as a certain chemical compound.

nucleus The very tiny, positively charged, central part of an atom that carries most of its mass.

photoelectric effect A phenomenon in which light can, under some circumstances, knock electrons out of atoms. Einstein's explanation of this effect led to scientific acceptance of the photon as a particle.

photon A particle of electromagnetic energy, such as light energy.

quantum electrodynamics (QED) A formulation of electrodynamics that accounts for quantum mechanical phenomena, such as the dual wave-particle nature of matter and energy.

quantum mechanics A field of physics developed to describe the relationships between matter and energy that accounts for the dual wave-particle nature of both.

reflection The phenomenon that occurs when an electromagnetic wave strikes an object and bounces off.

refraction The change of direction experienced by an electromagnetic wave as it passes from one material into another.

spectrum (plural: spectra) The mixture of colors contained within a beam of light, or the band produced when those colors are spread out by a prism or other device.

uncertainty principle Developed by Werner Heisenberg, a statement that nature provides fundamental limits on how well we can know two interrelated values, such as the position and speed of a particle.

wave function The quantum mechanical description that expresses the wavelike properties of a particle.

For More Information

Organizations

Boston Museum of Science
Science Park
Boston, MA 02114
(617) 723–2500
e-mail: information@mos.org
Web site: http://www.mos.org

The Franklin Institute
222 North 20th Street
Philadelphia, PA 19103
(215) 448-1200
Web site: http://sln.fi.edu

Lederman Science Center
Fermilab MS 777
Box 500
Batavia, IL 60510
Web site: http://www-ed.fnal.gov/ed_lsc.html
This museum is an outstanding place to discover
the science and history of subatomic particles. It
is located at the Fermi National Accelerator
Laboratory (Fermilab) outside of Chicago.

Magazines

American Scientist
P.O. Box 13975
Research Triangle Park, NC 27709-3975
Web site: http://www.americanscientist.org

New Scientist (U.S. offices of British magazine)
275 Washington Street, Suite 290
Newton, MA 02458
Web site: http://www.newscientist.com

Science News
1719 N Street NW
Washington, DC 20036
Web site: http://www.sciencenews.org

Scientific American
415 Madison Avenue
New York, NY 10017
Web site: http://www.sciam.com

Web Sites

Due to the changing nature of Internet links, the Rosen Publishing Group, Inc., has developed an online list of Web sites related to the subject of this book. This site is updated regularly. Please use this link to access the list:

http://www.rosenlinks.com/lsap/phot

For Further Reading

Billings, Charlene W. *Lasers: The New Technology of Light*. New York: Facts on File, 1992.

Bortz, Fred. *Techno-Matter: The Materials Behind the Marvels*. Brookfield, CT: Twenty-First Century Books, 2001.

Close, Frank, Michael Marten, and Christine Sutton. *The Particle Odyssey: A Journey to the Heart of Matter*. New York: Oxford University Press, 2002.

Cooper, Christopher. *Matter* (Eyewitness Books). New York: Dorling Kindersley, Inc., 2000.

Henderson, Harry, and Lisa Yount. *The Scientific Revolution*. San Diego: Lucent Books, 1996.

Narins, Brigham, ed. *Notable Scientists from 1900 to the Present*. Farmington Hills, MI: The Gale Group, 2001.

Bibliography

Close, Frank, Michael Marten, and Christine Sutton. *The Particle Odyssey: A Journey to the Heart of Matter*. New York: Oxford University Press, 2002.

Cropper, William H. *Great Physicists: The Life and Times of Leading Physicists from Galileo to Hawking*. New York: Oxford University Press, 2001.

Nobel Foundation. *Nobel Lectures in Physics 1901–1921*. River Edge, NJ: World Scientific Publishing Company, 1998.

Young, Hugh D., and Roger A. Freedman. *University Physics: Extended Version with Modern Physics*. Reading, MA: Addison-Wesley Publishing Co., 2000.

• Index

About the Author

Award-winning children's author Fred Bortz spent the first twenty-five years of his working career as a physicist, gaining experience in fields as varied as nuclear reactor design, automobile engine control systems, and science education. He earned his Ph.D. at Carnegie-Mellon University, where he also worked in several research groups from 1979 through 1994. He has been a full-time writer since 1996. He maintains a Web site at http://www.fredbortz.com.

Photo Credits

Cover, pp. 1, 3, 8–9, 14–15, 23, 24–25, 32, 40, 50 by Thomas Forget; p. 7 © Bill Sanderson/Science Photo Library; pp. 10, 16, 28, 31, 37, 38, 46, 52 © Science Photo Library; pp. 20, 36 © American Institute of Physics/Science Photo Library; p. 44 John Mclean/Science Photo Library; p. 49 © Bettmann/Corbis.

Designer: Thomas Forget; Editor: Jake Goldberg